Insecurity

How to Overcome Insecurity
and Increase Your Self-
Esteem to Eliminate Anxiety,
Jealousy, and Procrastination

Table of Contents

Introduction

Human beings are able to adapt to different settings. But despite their skills and abilities to acclimate to their surroundings, there are various factors that often inhibit their success.

Self-esteem, jealousy, procrastination, low confidence, anxiety, and relationship insecurities are just some of these factors. Although there are hundreds of pieces written on these subjects, applying what is expected in real life can be an uphill task.

This book contains proven steps and strategies on how you can improve your self-esteem, stop procrastinating, and stop being insecure, as well as tips for how you can apply them in today's life.

I believe the information shared in this book will help you be a better person after you finish reading.

Thanks again for downloading this book, I hope you enjoy it!

Chapter 1

Self-awareness: Trustworthiness and Safety

A lot of people find it difficult to just be who they are. Without the ability to define yourself and know who you are, you can experience a lot of inner turmoil. We human beings have certain things that we can't convey or express about ourselves around family members, at our workplace, or even to most of our closest friends.

But truth be told, nobody is absolutely perfect. We all have bright and dark sides, have questionable habits, strange thoughts, and issues that we haven't worked on which make us feel totally out of place.

There's no explanation needed for this: it's simply a part of life.

There is no more complex creature on this planet than we human beings, but above all we are stupendous. At the same time, we have a dark side hidden below the surface. This isn't just true for those who languish in their self-doubts. It is also true for those people who seem so incredibly secure in themselves. These people are considered positive, easy going, laid-back and nice, unlike the stingy, selfish and dismissive sorts. People who are secure with themselves are able to share their beauty, and they know how to deal with their negative side so it won't affect their day-to-day lives. This constant maintenance of oneself is a tremendous task only if you do it the wrong way.

It is vital for you to understand that your awareness is more important than your image. You might be aware of what you would like people to know about you and appreciate about you, but you might not be aware of what people think about you. Never at any given time think that the way you see yourself is the way people look at you. If there are things about you which you are aware of or are in denial about, others will see this as lack of self-awareness, and they will look at you as untrustworthy, unreliable, unapproachable, and unsafe. To be aware of oneself is indeed a big deal.

For example, you might be tall with a loud voice, and the two might be causing those around you to back away from such an imposing figure. If you are not aware, this will look like a normal thing to you. Unless you are aware of yourself, people will brand you without your being aware. The thing is, you will be unaware of the impact you will have on others. You might be causing others to feel insecure or uncomfortable. But when you have awareness about yourself, you will be able to make adjustments like lowering your voice, or be able to ask those who are around you to alert you when you start talking loud. This is to make sure that those who are around you don't feel insecure. Listen to others and not just the feedback of your mind. The main point behind this is to be aware. You will be able to adjust and fit into society and bond with those around you.

The best part is that when you work on self-awareness, those around you will be able to tell. Above all, to be independent, administer your own needs and take care of yourself, self-awareness is a key factor. And since you are always with yourself, take time and examine yourself.

There is one standard skill that emerges when it comes to self-awareness: listening. It is quintessential because it can be done anywhere and everywhere. It is a key that will unlock many doors for you beceause you can hardly make anything come through without listening. The trustworthy people we see around us always listen because they are aware of what it means to listen. Good listeners are those that know what to do, what to apply when and where, what to say and what not to say, and when they can be completely open.

To sum up, it looks like some people need to adjust more than others, but the fact remains, everybody is dealing with their issues in their own ways. Everybody's struggles are different, and now that we are living in a society where we are judged by superficial characteristics, it is a continuous journey to understand how best you can put yourself forward. Don't feel vulnerable in this journey. We are all travelers.

Chapter 2

Essential Ways To Build Self-Confidence

Confidence, as many know, is that feeling of self-assurance which arises from one's appreciation of one's own abilities. In life, there are many situations that we human beings face. Some are easy while others are not. Sometimes we succeed, and sometimes we fail, and all this contributes to who we are and what we do. Confidence is one factor that has led to the success or failure of so many people in life. You are faced with a circumstance, and in your mind you know you can make it, but the fear factor that emanates from your inner soul affects your focus. The result is that you do not trust your skills.

This is what has led to the majority of us to fail even in situations that should be easy to accomplish. But, as Hellen Keller said, never bend your head, always hold it high and look the world straight in the face. It's not too late for you to build self-confidence starting now.

If there is something in life that makes us happy, it is being able to accomplish something. It boosts self-esteem and self-confidence. Taking action and getting it done is what you simply need to do. Just sitting and procrastinating or just thinking about the problem will help nothing and will only make you feel worse. There are three recipes that can help you take action and get things done.

Lighten up your mind and do whatever you want to do. If you have a lighter state of mind, everything will be easier, and it will even be easier to get started. Don't force yourself; taking action should be a natural thing that you cannot wait to do.

Preparation is another key to self-confidence. How prepared are you? Many people have constructed horror scenarios of what might come next, and because of that they find themselves confused because they know nothing of what they are about to do. It is such a huge relief if you can prepare and educate yourself to avoid this sort of panic. For example, imagine you are going to deliver a speech to an audience. If you rehearse and write your speech prior to the day of delivery, and do some research, you will stumble on astounding techniques that will make you feel more confident, positive, and calm.

So, preparation will help you feel more confident and comfortable, and will help you avoid the panic that can immobilize your whole life.

I have come to realize one thing: failure is not permanent. The majority of us think that failing in something is the end of everything, but it should be the genesis of your accomplishments instead. This is because from failure you will learn something. In other words, it is a learning experience.

Failure will help you gain experience you could not get any another way. At times, we tend to learn from other peoples' mistakes and failure but sometimes it is good that we fail on our own so that we can learn a lesson and gain experience. Have you realized that you become stronger and more adaptable to situations when you fail? These are seeds of confidence that you are sowing in your mind so you will be in a position to tackle any situation that comes your way.

There is this norm in humans: we follow what others tell us. Who said that you cannot make it to destination A because so and so failed to do it? Don't listen to anyone who tells you that you can't reach point A or B, or you can't do this or that. Make up your own mind and go at everything. Never accept anyone else's idea that things are impossible or difficult.

Failure is required so that you will be able to know yourself better, grow strong, and figure out what you really want. After you uncover yourself, you will be more confident in what you do. Building self-confidence is a continuous effort that takes time. Maybe it is something that will never end, but the most important thing is that you can start now.

Chapter 3

Don't Be Afraid to Fail—Why not?

Situations happen in life where some goals are accomplished and some aren't. Nevertheless, everyone has his/her goals to accomplish. And despite the fact the goals may be pressing, there is no guarantee that everything will be successful. You have definitely tried something, and you ended up failing terribly, right? You are not alone, and you are neither the first nor the last. Chances are you are trying something new, you have the courage, you are gathering life experience, and you want to see where your strength will push you. You're definitely headed somewhere good.

You have set your priorities and your destination. Now you implement your priorities…only to find yourself in a hole. This means you have failed to accomplish your goal. Giving up isn't the solution, and if that is your choice, you are simply making yourself vulnerable to failures. Look around and decide what you are not willing to give up. The best part of it is that when you fail, you will learn something new. You will discover several opportunities that will reveal themselves after that bumpy journey.

Have you ever realized when you fail to accomplish a certain goal it is easy to feel exhausted? The feeling is natural, and if you deny it, then you'll be lying to yourself. It happens, and it is part of life. But you shouldn't allow the feeling to overwhelm you. Don't look for excuses to explain why you failed. If these excuses take hold in your mind, they will affect your focus, and it will be hard to let the feeling go. Failure should teach you to resist the anger that emanates after you have failed.

Failure gives birth to creativity. It goes without saying that if you are not willing to fail, then you will not be innovative. One way to sharpen your skills is to try again after you fail. You will not repeat the same mistake, but rather you will derive other ways to reach your destination. A fascinating thing is that—unlike adults who are worried about doing wrong—children always go after everything. When they fail, they move on to another solution. The fear of failure in mature people comes from the loss of natural flexibility and resilience as they age. They are not able to adapt to things as fast as they used to.

At some point in life, we should expect to fail. And once we fail, we gain more power to overcome tribulation. How? You will be able to break down the entire situation thereby recreating a new, different, and better solution. The more clearly you view the situation, the more encompassing and far-reaching reconstructions you are likely to make. If you can elevate yourself, you will be able to see the entire view of your journey. At the end of the day, everything changes and your experience will influence every situation you handle and every decision you make.

Take time and talk to those people who appear to have a successful life. They will give you a whole list of negative events or failures that got them where they are now. It's just like the way that maturity requires patience; you need to ride it out. It is just a matter of time, and you will remember it as something in the past. Never be afraid to fail. When you fail, wake up, dust yourself off, sweep the negative emotions out of your mind, and look

on the bright side. Try again and again. Never
allow failure to defeat you.

Chapter 4

Why Do People Get Jealous?

The genesis of jealousy is traced back in the holy book, and since then, this emotion has multiplied itself in the lives of humans. Jealousy can take you captive, especially if you allow it to take over your soul and mind. There are people who say it is an inborn emotion, which is true to extent because it is natural, but it can also be learned. Nevertheless, at some point in life, we get jealous, and there is nothing we can do about it.

Jealousy is two-way street. It is good because it is presumed healthy by some people because to them it means you treasure something or someone. Take, for example, being in love. When you realize that special love you have for your partner is being shared by another stranger, you will be overwhelmed by a twinge of jealousy. No wonder on several occasions you have seen people fight and do other crazy things.

This is why it is regarded as healthy, because without it, there is no relationship. Without jealousy, the relationship will come to an automatic end because it will be in your mind to turn tail and run. In essence, jealousy in a relationship means that you care for one another, and anything that comes between you will encounter ferocious resistance.

On the other hand, there are those among us who don't feel jealousy. You have seen such people around, haven't you? You have □. These people have a deeper inbuilt understanding, and they have a way of directing their negative emotions away. Once you allow negative emotions to bond with jealousy, you can hardly think positive. The two are a complete recipe to make one a prisoner of jealousy.

I should not talk about jealousy without mentioning envy. There is some chemistry between the two. Envy comes in when you see someone experiencing something that you would like to have. There is that wishful feeling in your soul like you want what they have, but the feeling does not necessarily lead to covetousness. The envious response in most cases leads to motivation and innovation. Jealousy is the combination of negative thoughts and a regressive state of mind. This is when in your mind you say, I want what he/she has, and until I get it, they should not have it. The difference is, instead of developing motivation, the emphasis in your mind is to demotivate others. You want to be like them or more than them. This is how jealousy becomes so calamitous.

Sometimes little feelings of jealousy are normal and understandable, but even if so, one should not allow it to escalate to chronic jealousy. If it does, it will interfere with your good character, and it will change your positive perception towards general well-being. To those who are prone to jealousy, there is a long road ahead of them to control this emotion consuming their minds and controlling them.

Jealous feelings in many societies are deemed as natural reactions when something you cherish is shared with someone else. Even those who have complete control of their emotions at times do feel insecure of losing a precious thing in their lives. This is normal, and it is part of human experience. Up to this point, you must have realized that fear and loss are also causes of jealous feelings. But now, the question here is how to get rid of this feeling?

It is not easy to pull yourself out of something in which you are deeply immersed. But you can start from changing the perception in your mind. Be open to communication and be honest with yourself. You have to be open about your fears and talk about them unflustered rather than confront loss with the limitations of jealous mindset. The majority fear to do this because it will make them vulnerable, but on the flip side, vulnerability is part of intimate relationships. So, the ball is your court.

Challenge yourself when you get jealous. Monitor yourself and see if you will find that seed that is giving birth to this feeling that you are going to lose that precious thing. Ask yourself why you would restrict someone else's joy, and if the same thing happened to you, how would you feel? It's upon you to control your feelings.

Chapter 5

Improve Your Self-Esteem

There are hundreds of articles, blogs, and newsletters that have been published on the subject "Self-Esteem" but it seems like the seeds fell on dry land rather than in a fertile oasis. There are those who firmly understand what self-esteem is, and there are thousands of individuals who are completely naïve about the subject. Among them, there are those who are struggling to understand what esteem is all about.

The most important thing in life is for you to understand how you think and feel about yourself. In today's life, the majority of people don't often love themselves, and this is an issue of self-esteem.

When you maintain a high level of self-esteem, you will be happy with who you are and how you live your life. Value your self-esteem and make it unshakeable.

Self-esteem has been proven to keep and maintain any healthy relationship. When you understand and are well aware of yourself, you will be able to tackle challenges and tough times better. You will be more of a natural giver and less needy. Personal drama will decrease, and baseless arguments and fights will be no more. This is healthy for any relationship, be it with your friend, your workmate, or your lover.

Many people are captives of their own lives. The worst part of it is that they are not aware that they are their own worst enemies. Maintaining a high level of self-esteem, you will realize that you deserve good things in life, and you will go after them when you are highly motivated. In addition to this, your life will become simple and happier. When you love yourself, everything will become simple. You won't feel less fortunate or blame yourself over simple life mistakes.

To enjoy all these benefits you will have to travel on a muddy road to reach your destination. Improving self-esteem is no easy task because the things that need to be corrected are the ones people rarely talk nor think about.

20

A good place to start boosting your self-esteem is your soul. You have at times found yourself cornered by your inner critic. We all have an inner critic, the source of all negative and destructive thoughts. You have seen in real life people who were polite become more aggressive, or how at the workplace your coworker who was always hardworking suddenly becomes dull and his work becomes questionable. So now you worry it might happen to you. At any given time when these thoughts come in your mind, you should change the way you view yourself and say "NO!" Replace this thought with something constructive and motivating.

Doing the right thing is another effective way of strengthening self-esteem. But what is the right thing? The right thing is simply the thing that feels right to you, deep down inside. It might be to wake up and go for a morning jog. It is not easy because of the ferocious resistance you will encounter from your inner critic, but you have to keep focus.

Kindness is a virtue, and there is nothing better than being kind to others. If you are kind to others, they will also treat you in a kind way. This sort of give and take which has a positive impact on one's self-esteem. Get out of your comfort zone and try something new. This way you will challenge yourself, and you will be able to learn something new. Trying something new will improve your performance.

Never fall victim to comparing yourself with others because you can't and will never be like them. If you do, then you have presented yourself as a victim of failure. Instead of comparing yourself, look at how far you have come in your own life and compare your past "you" to your present "you" and the "you" that you wish to become. How you have improved and how you can better your own results are enough to motivate you and improve your self-esteem.

Spend less time with destructive people and more with supportive people. It sounds easy, but to put it into practice is very difficult. We see in real life how successful people always associate themselves with other successful people. Supportive people always talk about success and encourage each other. Success always boosts self-esteem because you will always want to be better and to achieve more. You will remain motivated, and you will want to be a better version of yourself than you have ever been before. You cannot go back and start over, but you can start from where you are, be a better person now, and make a new ending. Start today.

Chapter 6

Dealing with Procrastination

Everyone is aware of the general expectations of life. Though these demands vary and at times are affected by several factors which lead to delay or failure of accomplishment, one emerging factor that is affecting how people meet their goals is procrastination. Some of us, if not all of us, spend a lot of time avoiding easy tasks. We tend to assume that since it is easy, we can watch TV and do it later. In the end, you have tons of tasks that have piled up waiting for you.

A little escape is harmless, but too much procrastination has a devastating effect on your daily tasks and goals at large. Most of the important things will not be done, and you will end up in an ocean of negative thoughts, which will cause your self-esteem to plunge. You will find yourself in an endlees spiral of depression.

It is possible to stop procrastinating and live your life in a normal and happy way. First, stop thinking too long about doing something; it becomes counter-productive. So, stop thinking and start doing. A small plan will help you execute what you want to achieve to perfection, but overplanning and overthinking will have the opposite effect. If you over-think, you will want to come up with a perfect plan, one which will have no mistakes and will not be rejected, one with no challenges. Yet, nothing like that exists.

According to Olin Miller, if you want to turn an easy job into a hard job, just keep putting it off. This idea was reiterated by George Claude Lorimer who said, "Putting off an easy thing makes it hard and putting off a hard thing makes it impossible." The two of them have hit the nail on the head because if you keep putting things off, you are only making mountains out of molehills, and at the back of your mind you think you are protecting yourself from pain. The more time you spend delaying something, the more it weighs on your mind.

Once you put something off, you will start thinking about the negative elements associated with it. This will make small issues grow into enormous ones. They will become like ghastly beasts that will ravage your life. To avoid this, stop thinking and just do it, no matter how you feel about it.

Face your fears. Procrastination is the triumph of fear. The majority of people procrastinate because they are afraid of success and the responsibility that comes with it. People are afraid to fail because they are afraid to look like fools. If you do this, one thing you should know is that you are responsible for what you do and no one else.

The first step is very important in every situation you find yourself in. If you have a goal or project that you would like to achieve, it might seem impossible. You are likely to shut down because you will be overwhelmed before you start. This is why you need to have a plan for the future, but your focus should be in the present. Just take the first step and remain focused. Doing so, you will defeat fear and negative thoughts. You will be resistant and remain motivated until the end.

When you wake up, you should start your day with the hard tasks, but many of us start with the easy tasks. Tackling hardest tasks will leave easy jobs to take care of themselves. And according to David Allen, much of the stress that people feel doesn't come from having too much to do but comes from not finishing what they started. Although there is no law that states you have to complete everything you start, not completing the task you started can leave you in a negative funk. Try and finish whatever you start as soon as possible so you can feel better about yourself.

Procrastination originates from one's mind, and without positive thinking, it is hard to overcome once it engulfs your mind.

Chapter 7

Start Empowering Yourself and Stop Comparing Yourself to Others

One ruinous habit is to constantly compare yourself and your life to other people. However catastrophic this habit is, we still see people comparing cars, houses, relationships, social popularity, and even money. Although it is natural to compare yourself to others and even envy them, if you start drowning in what you perceive as your inadequacy, rather than basking in those areas where you shine, then your focus is on the wrong thing.

You will erode your confidence and self-esteem right down to the ground, not to mention cause a lot of feelings of rejection within and conceivably outside of yourself. It requires some patience to stop this habit because it is something you have to work at.

First things first! The process of comparing yourself to others should start by how you view yourself. You should be fully aware of yourself and your thoughts. Failure to do this will result in you not being able to realize the concealed trouble. If you listen to yourself and your thoughts, you will be able to note the spring of your comparative behavior in your thoughts.

Learn to appreciate and be content with what you have. Just know that if you compare yourself to others, you can't win. This is because once you realize that your comparison is not working in your favor, jealousy and hatred strike. It is important you control your life and destiny. No one can control you apart from yourself. Make decisions that are best for you and those that will work for you. Don't look at what other people have, focus on who you want to be and what you want to achieve, not on buying a car because your neighbor's is new and shinier.

The way you think and behave towards those around you has a big effect on how you behave towards yourself and think about yourself. If you criticize others, you will do the same to yourself.

The best reaction here is to be kind to others and help them. This way, you will be kinder to yourself as well. Your focus should be on the positive things in yourself and those around you. Always appreciate the positive in others and in you. It is only through this that you will feel confident and comfortable with yourself and those around you.

Empower yourself and stop the habit of comparing yourself to others. When you compare yourself with others, you may view yourself negatively. This will give birth to negative thoughts. You need to replace negative thoughts with positive thoughts. Instead of immersing yourself in thoughts like "he made it because he has money" tell yourself, "I can do this or that and have my own cash."

Everyone is capable of achieving their goals so they can build confidence and improve their self-esteem. We are all heroes in our own way, and we are all failures at some point. Don't let your failure be a cornerstone for you to start comparing yourself with others. Build your own dynasty. Others will like you because of who you are as an individual, not because you are a duplicate of others.

Chapter 8

Overcoming Relationship Insecurities

Insecurity is one of the ingredients that causes a relationship to end. It is okay to feel insecure while in a relationship to a certain point. I believe the majority of us have been in a relationship before where things didn't work out, and you had to let it go. If your relationship is still strong, congratulations.

But those who have felt let down before or hurt in their previous relationships feel emotionally vulnerable when entering new ones. Their minds are tormented with questions like "Will they reject me? Have I done something to make them disappointed?" If you are one of those overwhelmed by these feelings, then you are a chronically insecure person.

You always see a problem where it does not exist. You become edgy and start looking for signs of things going wrong. Constant surveillance will be at your fingertips. Why did he/she say that? Who is this person being mentioned? Why did they laugh after I suggested we get together? All these are tiring, and if you always think like this, you are going to have a titanic time maintaining any relationship. But you can keep a healthy relationship. If insecurity is shattering your relationship, you are not alone, and you have to work your way out and bring things back to normal.

Trying to read your partner's mind is something you have to stop. Many of those in a relationship have this tendency of wondering what their partners are thinking about. This leads to anxiety which is not healthy in any relationship. Also, if your partner says something, don't interpret it thinking they mean something else. Mindreading is common in relationships where someone assumes he/she knows what the other is thinking. If you stop mindreading, respect will be the result, and everyone's privacy will be respected.

Relationships should not be compared. Just because your previous relationship didn't work out (maybe your partner was cheating on you or was abusive or left you) does not mean that your current relationship will be the same. Your new partner is not like your old partner, and comparison lead to destruction because of generalization. All women are gold diggers, or all men are lying bastards! Relationship comparison is a component of relationship breakage.

I have heard my friends saying "I want to know if she loves me" meaning they want to set a trap to prove this. What they fail to understand is that they are bringing tensions and strains to their relationships. Setting traps in a relationship is a sign of insecurity. We all have to live with uncertainty, and that is a fact, but insecure people will still feel insecure even when they are told they are loved.

Self-assurance is another factor that can help you overcome relationship insecurities. You don't always have to look up to your partner to feel secure. You have to challenge yourself and say even if the relationship comes to an end today, I can still move on. Challenge your fear and worries rather than accepting them.

A good relationship is that which is enjoyed by both parties, where they share resources and walk together to build healthy ways. I believe with this in mind, what you have is precious, and you will live to enjoy it.

Summary

Thank you again for downloading this book!

I hope this book was able to help you get rid of your anxiety; you are now in a position to strengthen your relationship, bond with others, and view daily problems from a different angle.

The next step is for you to start applying these tips in your daily life and prove to yourself and everyone else that you can be better if you want to. Although challenges might be there, you are the one to determine your destiny. So, start today and be a better person tomorrow.

Finally, if you enjoyed this book, please take the time to share your thoughts and post a review on Amazon. It'd be greatly appreciated!

Thank you and good luck!

Made in the USA
San Bernardino, CA
21 December 2016